DESTINY
FOUND HER FOR ME

DESTINY

FOUND HER FOR ME

Ed Ellis Jr.

If someone came to you with your life story, would you take it? If you asked me that a few years ago, I would have given you a different response then the one I would give this day. I look at myself through someone elses eyes today and I am glad I did not know. It would've caused me fewer pains, but I would have missed out on so much more. My wedding day I know would have been the same because I thought how that would have gone for years. Everything in my life has not been much of a surprise, until the day I met my daughter. On May 29, 2002 my wife and I walked into the hospital thinking we would go home early, because my wife thought she was not in labor. On May 29, 2002 at 4:18 I was looking at my daughter. I guess we were wrong?

I know I would like my daughter to not have any pain or hurt in her life but I would like her to know that she will not be the only one if she does go through it. Her father went through a lot before he met the one for him.

If you don't know who I am, don't be surprised. You are not the only one. I have worked in the place, that I work in now for the last nine years and I think people still think I am a different person then I really am. I was told life starts when you are born, but to me life started when I felt I was in love for the first time. My sister said it best, I am the "instant love pup". That is why I am writing, and now you will see what she meant by that. Example: I met this girl when I was seventeen years old. She really caught my eye, and I knew I had to talk to her. There was this little problem though, I was not sure that she felt the same. I decided to write this for her.

They tell me to follow my heart
But how can I follow my heart
When the heart my heart is following
Does not want to be found.

You always remember your first, that is what people tell me. Well, I think that is true. This was the first poem I ever wrote and it still gets me. I will never forget it and I will never forget her. I guess you figured we did not last. That's the way life is but at least I gave it a try. I wish I were told when I was born whom I would end up with, because that would"ve prevented a lot of heartache, for me.

I know that I am not shakespeare, and I never will be. I am just someone trying to understand this thing called love. I've met a few wonderful people in my life but the one hasn't found me. Every poem that I have written is about someone that I have met or wanted to meet in my life. What I mean by wanted to meet is, that I saw someone and they caught my eye, then I wrote something about that person, it could be you. I am the type of person that drives his car and looks around and wonders if she is the car behind me.

I went to school for a short period. School was definitely a growing experience. I wrote a lot of my poems sitting on a hill, looking over a lake, and the baseball field. When night falls in Mississippi it is a beautiful place. They definitely have beautiful scenery. That brings me to my next poem. I was not one who expressed his feelings but I had to for my best friend, Missy. I say my best friend because a friend is always there for you and she was definitely always there. When I found out my parents were separated she was there. When I found out my girl from home wasn't faithful she was there, you get the picture. I couldn't ask for anything more from this beautiful person. I wanted to give her something special to show her how great she really was to me. Don't worry I also bought her some presents for Christmas, but I did write what I felt.

This will be hard for me
I don't usually tell people how I feel
But I decided to make an exception for you
Time has never been on my side
And I want to tell you this right now
Before I leave for home
You have been the reason for my happiness
You made me forget all my problems
And you have made me happy
I hope I can do the same for you someday
Because of that I am writing this to say thank you

Missy was a good friend she kept me from going over the edge. She was the only one I could really talk to down there. I don't think she really understood me at times but she just sat there and tried. She even invited me home to visit her family. Her family ended up making me some Mississippi specials and boy where they good. I remember we just sat that night and watched 'men at work'. We then went outside and took a drive with mudd. This was one of Missy's friends and I had to call her mudd because I know that will Missy laugh when she reads this. We took a drive that night and her friend was driving a little to fast and she when off part of the road and hit a mud pile. From then on we called her mudd and the reason why there are two D's in mudd is because when Missy would say mudd it sounded like there was two D's. If you are reading this, Missy thanks again for being there and keeping me sane.

I have to tell you all something else that I find funny about Missy and I. I had a really bad night one night in Mississippi and of course Missy was there for me. I decided I would say thank you. I drove over to Missy house early in the morning with a rose in hand and a little note. I wasn't going to give it to her; I was just going to leave it on her car and drive away. I wanted it to be a surprise. I just wanted her to smile and then come over later to see me. Well I got to her stop sign and then it happened. Remember how I said you would always remember your first? Well I got in my first accident. I was just sitting at a stop sign and this guy was taking a right hand turn. Well he dropped his spit cup and he went to pick it up and he hit me. I couldn't believe it. Well mudd drove by the scene going to pick up Missy for something. She ran in the house to get Missy and in less then thirty seconds Missy was running up the street to see if I was o.k. Well she ran right past the rose. I had to point out the surprise. That day showed me even more how much of a good friend Missy was to me.

If I told you now how I feel
Would you walk away
I do not feel love because I do not know what love is
I can not say that I love you but I can say that I need you
I do not know what it is but love is a very important word to me
I have saved that word for a very special person
I am not saying that you are not important
But I just don't want to say it to quick
If I can say that I need you instead would you please believe me
Because if I lose you I may never know what love is
So please believe me I do need you.

I met this girl at a dance club. Her friend was a friend to my roommate, "Wild Bill Hippie". Wild Bill invited Drea over to our house one night with his friend amy. I couldn't believe it Drea seemed so nice I had to know more about her. I found out one bit of information that I liked more then anything else, she didn't have a boyfriend. She seemed so nice I thought she was out of my league. I told myself not to even think about asking her out, but Bill told me I should. I didn't ask her out that night but the next night I did and the reason was I lost a bet. I was playing golf with Bill that day and we were on my favorite hole. Bill was better then me in golf but he did give me a stroke. He bet me if I lost my favorite hole, I would have to ask out Drea, I lost. It didn't really matter anyway I just wanted an excuse to ask her out.

They haven't changed but my arms seem shorter tonight
My arms used to be able to touch my heart but tonight they can not
My heart is with you and there it will stay
Until I am back in your arms again
You have reached a part of me that no one has ever reached before
I am starting to understand the word love

At this time Drea and I had only spent about three weeks together as boyfriend and girlfriend. I didn't know what to expect from her because of that. I was going home for spring break and I wanted her to know that I would miss her. I actually wrote this on the plane on my way home. I was on Delta Airlines. The reason why I tell you what airline is I want to say thank you to the stewardess that gave me the pen and paper. I didn't have anything to write with and anything to write on. I was sitting there thinking and I knew that I wanted to write it down, but I didn't know what to do. I started to look around the plane for anything in the seats. This stewardess came over to me and asked me if I needed something. With a funny little grin I told her that I had something I wanted to write down but I didn't have anything. She smiled and said I think I can help you with that. Just to make sure I tell her again thanks. This letter was also a follow up letter to the one I wrote to her. She made me start thinking about something that I never thought about before.

When you have so much to say and you can not say a word it's hard
It seems like I can not look anyone in their face
Because I feel like I am telling them lies
The pain inside my heart is great
But I know that I can cause more if I release what I have
Is this to much for me to handle

The days seem to get longer and longer
Will I ever be able to release this pain
If I don't release it soon it will be the death of me

At this time I had been away from Drea for about three weeks. I know that I told her that I would be away for a couple of weeks and I had lied. I wanted to tell her that I knew I would be away for longer but I couldn't. My family told me that I was supposed to keep all of our problems quiet. I wasn't doing that well in school, so that wasn't the only thing. My parents thought it would be better if I went to a school that was closer.

I don't want to but I have to talk about the saddest day of my life
We had a fight that night
And I said I was going back to where I belong
I packed my things and said my good-byes
I then went over to say my last good-bye
I knew it would be hard but I thought I had to do it
As I was driving up to your house I knew I was wrong
But it had to be done
I can't believe I did it
I actually said good-bye to the only girl that I loved
I started my car on the first try
But I left you with a song
So you could remember me by
Now that song is on the radio
Who remembers who
I remember as I drove away
I wanted my car to fall apart
So I could turn around to tell you I was wrong and I loved you
I still remember that I wanted to stop at the bp gas station
To get you a fake rose
To tell you that like that rose my love for you will never die
But like I said I wanted to but I didn't
I let our love die when I said good-bye
Something did fall apart that night and it wasn't my car
And tonight I fall again as I hear that song

I decided I wanted to go back to visit Drea at school. When I was at home I got a job at Binni and Flynn's in Devon. I knew that my family did not want me to go back and that meant I needed to earn money for my travels. The place was a restaurant and I knew that I could make some money there. My sister had worked there before me. I had no experience and I didn't know if they would hire me, but thanks to this person named chic he gave me an opportunity. I don't know how to actually thank him though, because I don't know if going back to see her was the best thing. I decided I would go down there the week of her birthday. Her birthday was the last week of April. I was going to surprise her but I think I was the one that got the surprise. I decided I would go directly to her apartment she lived in. She was not there but I saw one of her friends at the pool from a distance. I decided that I would see if she was lying out. And to my surprise she was on the chair. Her back was to me and her friend had seen me first. I think I should have seen it there but I had on my blinders. She was surprised but not a good one. I decided I would go back to my apartment and visit my roommates. I told her that I would see her that night because I didn't want to ruin her plans that she had probably already made. I decided I would get her a cake for her birthday on my way home. I also decided to visit some of my friends. I was gone for seven weeks, so I had to do everything I possibly do in a couple of days. On my travels that day I saw one of my friends at the post office and he asked me to hang out with him. I decided I would for a couple of hours, until he received a phone call. I don't like to answer people's phones till this day because of this moment. He was doing something and he asked me to answer his phone. I knew this voice for seven weeks, and I couldn't believe I was in this situation. Till this day I don't know what went on if anything actually did go on, but I didn't care. I looked at my friend and laughed. I decided I should probably leave his place before I got mad. I went back to my place to visit with my roommates. When I got back to my place I got a phone call from the doctor, but I don't think she should've called. I don't think I was in the best of moods and my comments to her proved it. I told her that I bought her a cake but I decided my friends could have it instead. Two days I left Mississippi and I decided on my way out I would say my last good-bye to Drea. On my way to her house I thought I was doing the right thing, but on my way out I thought different. I stopped in tuscaloosa to write this poem. I was tempted to turn around but I didn't.

In everyone's life
They have felt what I am feeling this night
Everyone handles it differently
Some will cry
Others will want to die
Dying will help

You will never have to feel it again
Crying also will help
But someday you will feel it again
To me dying is not the answer
I have other feelings which I would like to feel again
So tonight I will cry over my feelings of loneliness

I don't know who or why I really wrote this poem, but I think this fits my life. I know that I was about to go out with Cougar and I just realized that Drea and I could not work. Cougar and I were talking at the time and I let her read some of my poems. She told me to keep with it and I should write her some. I guess I was thinking of her, and Drea. I had already heard some of her relationship problems and I told her mine. I thought if I would explain how I thought it should be, she would understand me better.

Real
That is what everyone wants?
They want it to be real
They will do anything to make it that
No matter how much it hurts
But when it's real you don't have to do anything
You don't even have to say anything
You just know it is
Its what you wanted; it's real
Nothing needs to be done
All you have to do is keep it that way
Because you never want to lose
Something that is real

Cougar was dating a person when I met her and she told me that she wasn't happy. She told me that she was trying too hard and she didn't know if it would be worth it. I used to sit and talk to her for hours and that's how I came up with a few poems. I told her that love was a crazy thing and not many people know what it really is, but I don't think it should be that hard for her. She told me to write something down that would explain it better, and this is what I wrote.

Every time that I hear that word
It doesn't matter who it comes from

I think of you
It was a word that I never thought would be said
The way things were going why would I want to say it
But time brought around a change
And I could not stop it
I had to say that word to you
But understand
I didn't want it to be forever
When I said that word to you it came out wrong
I know what that word means
But I do want to see you again
So please
Don't let good-bye be good-bye

After I left Mississippi I thought a lot about Drea. I was wondering if I did the right thing or not. I wanted to let her know that she meant a lot to me and I couldn't help but think about her. I wanted to see her again at this point but my pride would not let me. I figured if I gave her this letter, she would understand more about me and how I felt. I didn't want us to end the way that it did. I sent this poem in the mail and she did receive it, but the response that I received was not the one I wanted. She told me that she loves the poem, but we were over.

So many times I tell myself she doesn't love me
And she does not care
I never tell her this but I do
I have even convinced myself that she doesn't
I know I should not do this but it's my way of protecting myself
I never get hurt this way in my eyes
But I am wrong and I have noticed this
Because of my feelings for her now
I have to change
I will no longer tell myself that she does not love me
I will let myself know that she feels what I feel
And that feeling is love

Cougar kept me writing; because she knew that is the way I would express my feelings and not be afraid. She used to ask me everyday if I had a new poem for her or just a new poem. I don't think she realized how important she was in my life. She really helped me get over Drea. She would also try to make me express more of my feelings. I think this poem shows that I was starting to let more out. At the time it was the only way I could show my feelings. I was to wrapped up in the past and I needed to let go, and Cougar was the only thing I wanted and could see in my future.

The pain inside my heart
I know that no one will ever see
There is no reason for me to show it
When I'm with you it all disappears
I don't know how you do it and I really do not care
As long as my pain is hidden
In time I will tell but please don't ask
Now I know if I had to tell I could tell you
And like our song says no one has touched me so deep, so deep, so deep, inside
In your arms that's where I like to be
And that's were my pain disappears and my heart belongs to you

Cougar asked me to write a poem that would have our song in it. Like I said she wouldn't let me stop writing. She knew that I liked to do it and she definitely liked reading them. I wanted to tell her the problems that I was having with my family but I really wasn't aloud to. I couldn't tell her but I knew if I was actually going to tell anyone it would be her. I know that she wanted to know but she told me that she understood and she said whenever I was ready she would be to. She stuck by me no matter what. That song, by Paula Abdul, was definitely a fitting song for us. I don't think anyone touched me as much as she did. She knew me more then I knew myself.

I can't believe I didn't let this enter my mind
I thought I was the only one with this problem
And with you it didn't occur to me
That you had a past too
You told me how this one hurt you
Then how much you loved that one
And you made love to him
Because you thought you loved him
But he didn't love you back
How this one cheated on you
How did I let this slip my mind
Now that I see that you have lived as I have

I ask for you to share your memories with me
So we can make it better
Tell me how you feel
Tell me what you love
And then we can make our memories
Together.

I knew that Cougar was there for me, but one day I wondered if I was actually there for her. I told her about my past and I thought I listened to hers, but for some reason one day this poem came to me. I wanted her to know that if we would tell each other everything we could be even closer. I wanted her to know that I would like to know everything. I didn't care what came out of her mouth I could take it, as long as she could accept mine. I knew she would accept me and I wanted her to know I would do the same.

Tonight I feel pain
Pain that I will never forget
You haven't left but you told me
You love me for the first time
And I believe you
But the pain is that I am not there with you
All I can think about is when I will be next to you
And I can tell you the same
So you can believe me as I believe you

I was home for spring break and Drea was away. She was in Florida. She was out drinking one night and she called me at home. She just wanted to tell me that she loved me. I never told anyone that I loved her with understanding that word. I remember I was shocked to hear that she loved me. I had a baseball in my hand at the moment and a pen. Yes, I wrote this poem on the baseball. I think that was the only time that I heard those words from her. I think she was a little drunk. I wanted to believe that she loved me, but I also wasn't sure. I was afraid to know the truth.

A hug
It is usually used to show that you care
Or to help someone over their pain
I thought
A beautiful sign of affection used to your advantage

When you gave me your hugs it wasn't to show me that you cared
And it wasn't used to help me over my pain
Your hugs were given to tell me that you cared
But you told me you cared to my ears
Not to my face
You knew what you were doing
It went all through my body
You even sent chills down my spine
But now as I look at you
Your face tells me what your whispers would not
You didn't and don't care

I don't usually write anything that is angry poems, but I did say usually. I met this girl at Kutztown University and I thought that she liked me, but as you see I found out that she didn't. I didn't understand why she only told me that she liked when she hugged me. It wasn't good to find out the truth. This is the time that I wish that I had eyes in the back of my head. I would've seen that she didn't feel anything. If you ever had this happen to you, you would know that this doesn't feel good. If this has never happened to you just be aware, because it just might. If anyone can't look you in the face you might want to back up and take a better look. It's good to feel loved, but it can't be one sided.

Because I love you I walk away
One day we will all meet again
I wasn't planning on leaving
But no one ever plans this
I don't know how I entered this world
Now I don't know where I am going
All I know is that I have loved
I have even laughed
And I have also cried
Nothing was better than the feeling of being alive
No one should worry no one should cry
In time you will forget
But I will never forget how much I loved
Now it is time for me to go
I leave you with this
War does not settle anything
It just puts someone's love where I am today

And it might just be yours
I entered this world in peace
I left this world in peace
Let's let everyone do the same

I was in Mississippi when I wrote this. I was watching the news with Suddam and the Persian Gulf War. I looked at all the people and just wondered. I put myself in the everyone's shoes for a second. They were over there fighting and for what. I know that there was a reason but why did it come to this, couldn't people see that war does not need to exist. I know that we all have our differences but we don't need to kill. You don't know what the person you are fighting has to lose, and what another has to go through if they lose that person. I know that if I was at war, and I did not return, my family and friends would be hurt. I think we should think about that when the thought of war is brought up.

Tonight I ask
I want you to come closer
Closer than you have ever been
Tonight when I reach for you
I will reach with all of me
My heart is open
And I am willing
Willing to let you inside
Now all I ask is for you to do the same
Open your heart

When I was at Kutztown I met this girl and I thought that if I would open up more she would want me more. I was a young person you have to give me some slack. I think I surprised her with this poem. I think I thought she would like it but she was not that type of person. I thought at the time that anyone that you met was the possibility they could be the one. I still think the same to be honest. When people tell me that you never know I believe them.

I'm trying
Trying in my way to get your attention
Usually for me words are easy
But with you I don't know
I can't seem to say it
So for now this word won't be spoken

But as you see I said for now
Hopefully soon it will be spoken freely
But for now it will be written
Hi.

I saw this girl when I was at Kutztown that caught my eye. I was afraid to say anything to her, because she seemed to be out of my league. I don't think I would remember her if I saw her today but those days I couldn't forget her face. I had one of my friends drop this off in one of her classes. She told me that she liked it, till this day I still laugh at myself for writing this and actually giving it to her. I still think that this was a corny letter but I wanted to take a chance. In everyone's life you will look like a fool, but who really cares, it was definitely worth it.

I can't see tomorrow
Without looking at today
Though today looks bright
Tomorrow will come
You are here today
But tomorrow I will be gone
I love to be near you
You are the reason
Why I wanted today to come
I have realized that time moves
And I only have so much of it
I have to use all of it tonight
Tonight I will hold you
And I will love you
When tomorrow does come
You will then know
I will be waiting for the next tomorrow
That we will have together
And I hope it's soon

To understand this whole poem you need to know a few things. My friends had planned a trip for new years, and they wanted me to go. They wanted me to go to Daytona, Florida. I told her that I was not going with them. I wanted to spend that new year with her, but my ex-girlfriend and I got into a fight right before Christmas. I didn't know why I did it but that night I was mad and that's when I told the guys I would go. I didn't know what to do because that week my

ex-girlfriend and I got back together. I had one problem I already gave my friends
the money to go to Florida. As I think back I should've just stayed home. The
whole time that I was gone I thought of her. I didn't want to go and she told me
she didn't want me to go either. I never gave her this poem. I wanted to forget that
I went and for her to do the same.

Time goes by
And that's when I noticed
That time never stops
At times I wish it would fly
Then there are times I wish it would stop
But without it I would have never met you
You have given me reason to look for tomorrow
When tomorrow comes I will be there
That's when I wish time will stop
So I can show you your importance to me
When I hold you
I just want you to be loved
I don't have a goal
But I do have time
So as I look at my watch today
I wonder how long it will take
Because I want to hold you
To give you what you deserve
And to receive what I need
You in my arms

The night I was leaving for Florida I wrote this poem. My heart told me to tell
her how important she was to me, but she kept on telling me how disappointed
she was in me. I knew that I would miss her, the minute I left. She bought me a
watch and I couldn't stop looking at it. I never really wore a watch, but I couldn't
help to wear this one. I don't think this one worked at times though; it seemed
to stop when I wasn't looking. I kept on thinking of her and wishing this watch
would go faster.

Where should I start
Do I give all that I can
Or should I start off with a hello
I dream about that day

And I hope for it to be tomorrow
But each day passes
And that tomorrow passes also
You haven't entered my sight
And I wonder if you ever will
But I keep my thoughts to myself
I want only you
To hear my thoughts and my dreams
I keep on giving and never receiving
Though people think I have no feelings
They haven't seen the real man
Should I show them
My heart says he wants to wait
And to me that is the one that controls this man

I was dating Dave's girl and I knew that I was not happy. I met this girl and she seemed to understand how I felt about relationship. When I met her I knew that I didn't want what I once had. I also heard that Dave's girl might be looking for something else. My ex-girlfriend made me feel wanted and I wanted to feel that way. I took my ex-girlfriend to a movie and I told her exactly the way I felt and she felt the same. That is when I knew that I needed to be with her.

When I saw you, my eyes I didn't want to blink
Because I was afraid that you would not be there when they opened
Unfortunately they could not hold on
I had to close them
But I opened them as soon as I could
And there you still were
I didn't want this vision to end
But your day was not over
And you had to move on
Now I wonder if I will ever see you again
My only hope is my past
I closed them once before and you were there
Tonight my eyes remember today and look forward to tomorrow
That you, my vision, will reappear once again
I haven't learned which one works the best
So tonight I will try them all
I will bake a cake and blow out all the candles

I will put all my pennies on heads
I will cross all my fingers
I will get down on my knees
And I will even take a walk to look for a four leaf clover
Maybe if I do all of that
You will walk back into my sight
That is when I will tell you what your sight has done for mine

Remember how I told you early that it might be about someone I didn't know or never met. I was working the bar at Bennigan's with a girl named Jill. I couldn't believe how many people were there that day, but only one person caught my eyes. Her name was Mindy and she was the reason for this poem. She made a comment on how nice that I was to everyone, but the only one I wanted to talk to be her. I wanted to ask her more about her life but she didn't have the time. I thought maybe she would come back and see me again but she did not. I guess someone else was taking good care of her. I wonder today if she will be reading this, and maybe she will realize she definitely has something special.

The pillow is the only thing I can hold tonight
Tonight when I roll over to turn out the lights
I notice that I am already in the dark
In the dark about how I feel about me

In my thoughts, I know you are
In my dreams, I know you will be
And in my life, I hope you will stay

But all of these feelings are kept
Kept because I'm afraid to tell you how I feel
But in these words you will know
That you are a part of me
And I want to show you this part that has been kept

In my thoughts, you are
In my dreams, you will be
And in my life, please stay

I'm afraid to love someone who just wants to be loved
It doesn't matter who it may be

They just need someone to hold
Holding I can do
But I can give so much more
I hope you have realized this
Because when you are away I will be thinking
Thinking of the time we spent
And I hope you will too
I trust you will not let another enjoy the time
Time that means so much to me
And I wish that one day you will stay

In my thoughts, you always are
In my dreams, you always will be
And in my life, I want only you

I wrote this poem when she went away for college. She went to Millersville University and I knew that we were drawing to a close. I enjoyed being with her and I hope I would get a better feeling on what she was thinking about our relationship. I didn't give it to her when she left though, I waited, two years to give it to her. She went to college and did her thing and we somehow remain friends. When they say better late then never I don't think they meant this. I think it was better that I waited though she would have never talked to me again if I gave it to her when we only dated for three months. She told me that she really did like it two years later. I call her Dave's girl because she just got out of a relationship with him that lasted three years. I didn't want to let all of my feelings out for a rebound.

As I talk to you tonight I remember what I thought I forgot
I remember that we shared some good times
And that I really did care for you
Nothing will ever be the same but some thing's will never change
We can never go back and change what went wrong
But the dreams I have of you will always be strong
I have tried to get back to you and love you
But you know that is not possible
We never fought and said it was over
But we both just knew
We never saw one another when I was a thousand miles away
We kept in touch by this phone
And tonight it's the only thing that keeps me from telling you how I feel

I told you before that I didn't want to leave you
And tonight I know that I never did
Because the phone keeps us in touch
I may not be able to touch you
But when I hear your voice I remember the way you felt
You may have begun a new life and I should begin mine
But for now I just want to remember what once was
So keep talking so I can keep remembering

When I was at home from Mississippi State I thought I was over Drea. I decided I would call her to see how she was doing and to try being friends with her. I don't think you can be friends with someone that you care for, because you will hurt in the end. I didn't want to hear about her love life, but that's what was on her mind those days. She was going through some hard times. We ended up losing track of each other after I wrote this poem, because I knew that I cared too much. I could not forget that she meant a lot to me.

No not again
It's been hurt before
I don't need the human eye to hurt it once again
For now I will keep it hidden
So before you tell me I don't care
And tell me I don't have a heart
Think again and look deep
It's there but I don't want it hurt
It still hasn't healed from the last one
I now understand why an arrow is always put through a heart
When people say they are in love
If not touched the arrow will not hurt
But when removed the heart bleeds
It then leaves a scar that can't be repaired

I just broke up with a girl and I had met someone later that month. She told me that I seemed drawn back. I know that she was right because I knew that I was that way. I think whenever you date someone new they take away something else from you. That is why I wrote on this poem to everyone that I have ever dated and to the people I will date. Just because someone seems to be drawn back it does not mean that they don't have any feelings. I know the reason why there is an arrow, but I made up my own reason for it, and I hope everyone sees my point of view.

Can they tell
That you are the one
That you are my thoughts
No one seems to see
But only you have control
I can walk down any street
Only to see you
Though you may be with him
I can see right through
The love you feel for me
I feel the same
But I am with her
To be with someone
And to feel alone
Is a feeling I do not like
Im holding back

I met this girl one-day and I knew that she was someone I wanted to get to know. I thought about her a lot and we even had a song for each other. I kept it quiet from everyone, because I knew that we both had someone else in our lives. I think everyone in his or her lives will meet this person. They make you think about them when you know you shouldn't. The good thing and maybe a bad thing are I didn't do one thing. She had to leave and I let her go without telling her. Maybe one day I will tell her, but I don't think it will make a difference. She will always be a happy memory and paula cole's song will always make me smile.

To all I the people I see
I wonder
What they may be
Or who they can be
Everyday I see people
But not too many stay in my mind
I always want to say
What I really feel
But something
Always holds me back
Maybe it's that
What I'm feeling doesn't last long enough
But then there's you

I saw and remembered you
You may not be for me
And I may not be for you
But someone has to tell you
What I am feeling
And what everyone
Can clearly see
You are beautiful

I remember the day I wrote this. I couldn't believe that I could be taken by surprise so easily. She came in to my work for a job, but I thought she could help me more then I could help her. She was late but in my opinion she was right on time. I tried to help her understand the job but I couldn't keep my mind off of the possibilities. Everything that she did made me laugh. I remember every time she would be thinking she would raise her hand from the table and close her fist. The things that I remember make me laugh. The little things that people do will always be more lately.

When I look at you
I can't seem to stop
You have that something
That makes me want to be near you
I may not know what it is
But I do want to find out
I feel like I have seen you before
Though it may be strange
Strange is what I feel
These words may not change anything
You could only be only a sight
But I have to tell you now
To my eyes you are a nice sight

The second day that I met this girl I had to train her, but I still was a little sidetracked. I had to flip a coin to see which one of the trainee's I would train. I still remember that the coin was heads, and she got to train with me. She seemed happy to get me, but I think I was happier. She asked me so many questions about myself; I started to think she was a little interested in me. That was good because I definitely felt the same.

I am always writing
But what is it that I am writing about?
Have I ever seen it?
Have I let it pass?
Have I ever been in it?
And if not
Will I ever find it?
Someone has mentioned the word to me
But today that word seems unclear
When I looked at you
I didn't want to stop
You have something
That makes me want
Want to be near you
I may not know what it is
But I do want to find out
I feel like I've seen you before
Though it may be strange is what I feel

I told my friend Bobby about this girl at work and he said he wanted to meet her. I told him that one-day he would get the chance but I couldn't tell him exactly when. He really didn't like that answer, so he said we should go to my work that night. She was training that night and he thought there was no better time then the present. There was a baseball game on TV and he said that was a good front. We ended up going and she was happy to see me. We then went to Uno's after the game and we sat there and talked to her and her friend. That is when I asked her to go to my game that weekend. She thought I was interested in her friend, but she found out that night who I really wanted.

I read what you had to say
But reading that told me that you don't know me at all
I guess that letter was supposed to heal me
Over what I was feeling
But it did nothing
It did help me make my decision, though
My relationships need trust
Yes you are right
We have gone through a lot in the past

But I am not ready to climb once more
This always seems to happen
And after reading your letter
I noticed you never understood
I think it's better for the both of us to forget
In my eyes my future is no longer the same
I will be looking in a different direction

Dave's girl and I were seeing less of each other and I didn't like it. I always went to see her and she didn't seem to mind that. I wanted her to realize that I wanted more. I needed the same that I was giving her. I finally told myself that she and I wouldn't last. I felt something more and I needed to find someone that would feel the same. That is when I decided I would go and find someone else. I took a long look at what I gave and what I received, and it was not in my favor. I know that you should never expect anything, but sometimes you should be on the receiving side. I took a look at what I did for her on Valentine's Day one year when we were friends. I went to her school because we both wanted to have a Valentine's Day. I know that we were friends, but I wanted her to have a special day. I bought her a dozen variety roses, four were red, four were pink, and four were yellow. I took her out to dinner, and I dressed up nice for her. I know that she liked cross-stitch, so I even cross-stitch something for her. It took me two weeks to do that thing, and that made me realize how hard that stuff was. I think we had a great time, but when I went home I didn't receive any phone calls from her for about two weeks. I found out later on that she ended up going out with someone later that week. She read her diary to me when we became friends that summer. At the end of her entry that day she wrote "sorry ed." I could never let that one line ever leave my ears. I guess it's my turn to say I'm sorry.

I never thought a kiss could hurt
But yours does
Not physically but mentally
Now I need and want it
But I can't have it
You have said good-bye
And you will never be back
You told me we have nothing in common
I thought we did
I know that I cared for you
But know I am finding out that you didn't
How can this be

I guess my sign of affection
Didn't move you like yours did me
Why is that?
Questions are all I have
And they will never be answered

I wrote this poem to follow up the hug poem. I wasn't actually talking to that girl anymore, but I still wrote the poem. I wasn't planning on giving her this poem it was just for my own use. It helped me realize, I was alone, and on the way I felt. This wasn't meant for "keen-eyes" but it was a follow up to the hug poem. I meant this for Dave's girl. Every time that we needed each other we were with someone else. I never realized how much that hurt me. She meant a lot to me and I felt I was alone in that feeling.

Watching me grow
But now needing my strength to move
Laughing at my jokes
But now crying in bed
Walking the dog
But now watching the dog being walked
Wanting to see me married
But now hoping to see tomorrow
What brought me here
Is slowly losing strength
And I don't know what to do
If I could I would give it all
My blood
My heart
And my soul
She did it all for me
I took her blood
She gave me a heart
And with that she gave me life
All my strength can be hers
Because without her all my strength is gone
But I know in my heart it's not her time
I can't imagine Christmas without her
Please hear my Christmas wish
Give her my strength and love to heal her

My mother got sick right before Christmas and I had no one to talk to. I had some problems dealing with it and I only could talk for so long about it to people. I didn't have anyone that I could really count on so my journal became my best friend. I wrote this so someone would hopefully hear me. My mother means a lot to me and I'll tell you why . . .

I was ten years old and it was the middle of the baseball season. My mother missed her first game of the year. She ended up missing a lot more, but that when I knew she was sick. She would never miss a game. She ended up going into the hospital for a couple of months. I would go visit her after every game and even if she couldn't ask she would try to point at my uniform. I would have to tell her if we won and how I did. My season ended and she was still in the hospital. I made the all-star team and we would only have about two more weeks left to play. My mom became a little antsy. She really wanted to go to one of the games before the season was over, but the doctor said she had at least a week left in the hospital. I only had one more game left and my mom had at least four more days left. She asked the doctor if she could go to the game and then she would come back that night. You have to understand that she had a tube through her nose for food. The doctor said if you don't mind pulling that thing out of your nose yourself I will let you go. My mom actually started to do it. Her doctor was just kidding with her but he then realized how important it was to her to be there. He okayed it but she had to be right back after the game. We got to the game an hour before game time. My dad had to wheel my mom to the stands. She didn't want anyone to know that she was sick. I had the best game of the year that game. She looked so happy that day, but I think I was the happiest because when we got back to the hospital the doctor noticed how happy she was and her counts were even a little better. It wasn't any miracle it was just a mother and her child. Thanks for coming to my game mom . . . .

Everyday I feel
What no one has felt
And every night
I hurt like no one knows
I tell everyone that I am fine
But I only know that I am wrong
I hurt the one that loved me
I want the words
The words that will bring you back
Though I have tried
It hasn't changed a thing

Only we have seen
What people have dreamed about
I can't help but dream
That one word will change
Change what you feel
Because you are the one
The only one that I want
So what are the words
The words that will bring you to me

The girl that I couldn't take my eyes off of, left. I hurt her and she needed to get away from me. She told me numerous times, that one day I would see what I did. It's too bad that it was too late. She couldn't stay with me anymore and I could never get her back. I thought there was a word or words but I was wrong she had enough. When you hurt someone that much there is nothing that will bring him or her back. It will not matter how nice you can be; she will always remember how mean you were.

As I walk across the floor I find the dance
that we once had
I stood at the same spot that we danced for hours
The music still plays but the dance is over
Or has it just begun?
I now have a memory which I didn't have before
I think I would rather have the dance
That dance that lasted for hours
Not the one that will last forever in my mind
I now see that you are on the floor but not with me
You have brought someone else to the floor that once was ours
I don't know how this has happened but time has changed
As we danced on the floor for hours a person stood where I stand
I now know what it feels to be that guy and the one that hurts
I wonder if he had the same thoughts that I have tonight
Did he want to start another dance with you like I do
Well my thoughts are only mine I will stay quite
like he did
The new guy smiles like I once did and I am glad for him
I see him glance over to me as I did to him
I know what he is thinking

And I just hope one day he does not know
what I am thinking
Because he will then know about the dance
that never ends

I saw an old girlfriend at a club with a new man, and he saw me. It was really weird to see things reversed. I knew exactly what everyone was thinking and it seemed really weird. I don't know who the other guy was that was watching my ex and I that night but I am now sorry I did what I did. I know that these things happen but I wish that I wasn't involved. I understood what they mean when they say that things will come back to you. If you do something to someone you will receive it back.

Without
That's all anyone ever talks about
Without me knowing, I fell in love with her
Without me knowing, she took everything I have
Without me knowing, she was seeing another
Why does this happen
I don't like without's
I don't want to know that I will be sad without you
I don't want to know that you feel what I feel without me knowing
Tonight I will take a chance and look for the smile
That comes from knowing
Knowing what you know
Knowing the feeling of love

I was listening to someone's conversation, and I really got annoyed. I never understood why people just do not take chances. I know that it might not but its better than wondering if you could have been happy. The reason I started writing this whole book is because I took a chance and it did not work, but I knew that I had to try. I was happy for the time though. I told myself after I wrote this poem I would not let myself say those words anymore.

When you look to your left you see nothing
When you look to your right you see the same
But when you look behind you there he stands
As you he has been hurt before
That is why he is not in front of you
He is afraid to take any chances

But if you show him that the love you have is real
He will be there for you
As you he has a lot of love to give.

I wrote this poem for Cougar, so she could understand me just a little more. I wanted to be there for her, but I was also afraid if I was, I would be alone. I found this to be a good poem about myself. I would be there for her but I did not want to get too involve. I would do anything for her to make her happy, but I was always a step behind. I thought that would keep me from being hurt. I found out later that the more I did the more I got involved, but with her I did not mind. She made sure I remained happy.

The hold
When I saw you in that room
You put it on me
The hold
It could cause me pain
But there is none
I can feel it though
And it feels good
I wish I could tell you
But I can't
You and I are with others
And that hold could cause pain to them
That is where my pain has begun
You with another and the hold
That he has and I want

I just started seeing this girl and I realized I was seeing the wrong one. Her and I didn't really have that much in common but we just needed each other. I remember lying down on a couch watching a movie and the other girl came in. I tried to hide because I felt that if she would see me I would never have a chance with her. It sounds bad but the girl and I really were more than just friends seeing friends. I knew we wouldn't stay together and she did too.

As he tells me
That I will no longer be able to do that
I remember the promise I made
We were all alone

You looked in my eyes
And asked me to promise
Promise that I wait
Because you were scared
I made that promise
And that made you smile
Usually my promises are good
But that one wasn't
And now I will pay
There's nothing he can do
He doesn't know how long I have
How can I tell you?
Should I tell you?
Im afraid to go
Because I will never see that smile
If I tell you my promise would be broken
And if I don't tell you
I would have left here with a lie
A lie to the only one that matters

I wrote this poem when I found out that my mother was sick. I was dating someone at the time and I felt very uncomfortable around her after I heard how sick my mom really was. I told her I would be with her forever and looking at my dad and how sad he was I thought I could be wrong someday soon. I felt like I was feeling the same as my mother. I hurt her because I couldn't live with dying. I know I was not sure of what would happen with me, but I didn't want someone to be hurt. I don't think anyone knows his or her outcome in life, and I now know you can't worry about it. You will never be happy if you are afraid. I was afraid to hurt the one that I loved. I wasn't sure if she could handle what my dad had to go through.

The tears that fell down when you left are back
But not the way that they were
They are tears of love
I was thinking about giving up on our love
But you have drawn me back again
I am so glad that you have
This time it will be better

Because I will not be afraid to tell you how I feel
I care a great deal about you and this time I want forever
So now it's time
Will you marry me

I let this one go because I was afraid. I wanted her to have her fun, and I thought I would be in the way of that fun. I saw her everyday and I couldn't let her know how I felt. Everyone else knew that I wanted more but she needed me to go away. I know that I should've said something but something held me back. I never really cared for anyone like I cared for her, and I never thought this day would come that I would want to say those words. I thought it's hard for me to tell someone that I love him or her, but I realized that asking someone to marry you is harder. It's true if you think that three words are hard, that fourth is a killer. I never gave her this poem, because I knew in my heart the answer would be, no.

Can you please walk out of my life
I never wanted any woman more then I want you
But I know I can't have you
You mean more to me then I could possibly show
When you are around the memories are too much for me to handle
I need you and I want you
But if you knew you wouldn't want me
When you are around you're all that I want in this world
If I end up with you I would believe in destiny
But as you can see right now
You want to be free but I need to have you
So please, walk away

I followed this poem up from another poem. I couldn't tell this person that she meant everything to me. Everyday that I saw her I wanted to tell her, but she needed time apart from me. I know that she wanted to explore what else was out there, and I wanted her to only explore the possibility of us. I couldn't take looking at her seeing what else could be. I didn't realize how important this person was to me until she left. She and I would talk all the time, and I realized that she had me if she wanted me. We had so much in common and I was the only one that could see that. I do believe in destiny. Everyone has someone that was meant for him or her they just need a little help.

Does he have to leave or is he returning?
The picture tells all
His hands are controlled by his suitcase and pocket
He has no time to hold or to be held
But he takes time out to show that he cares
He looks into her eyes and leaves her with a kiss
But the train needs to move
So the day can go on
He will remember the kiss and wait for the hug
When his day ends the train will return
That's when the suitcase will be dropped
And the pocket will release the hand
He will have time to hold and time to be held
Everyday is the same
The picture tells all, they found love

I really like those pictures from Kim Anderson, and one day I looked at one of them I wrote a poem about it. It was a picture of a little boy giving a kiss to a little girl at the train station. I wrote the poem and I talked about that poem at work with one of our guests. Well, she wanted to take a look at that poem, because it reminded her about her situation. I brought that poem and picture in to work one day. She really liked it and asked me if she could have a copy of that and the picture. I got her a frame and put it all together. The funny thing of it all is that they ended up getting married at our store. I know that the poem was not the reason, but every year on that date I remember that one of my poems touched someone enough that they wanted it. I hope that every time she reads it, she remembers how important love can be.

Where to begin and would I ever end
That was my problem writing my Christmas
lists in my past
I was told that Christmas brings you what you want
Not what you need
I might have needed new socks but a new bike is what I wanted
When I was younger I always woke up for Christmas
with a smile
I was usually the first one down the stairs
Because I knew every year that Santa knew what I wanted
I wasn't the type of person to ask for too much

But I also wasn't afraid to ask
And this year is no exception
But this year is definitely different
This year my wants and my needs have come together
Today I write to Santa again
This year my list is short and sweet
I have told her that I need her
But this year I have to her that I also want her
She is my Christmas list
I ask for nothing else
Santa couldn't give me anything else in the world that would make me smile
more
This year I want to be a kid again
Running down the stairs with a smile
Please Santa
Grant me my Christmas wish . . . .

One of my ex-girlfriends was with someone else during Christmas and I thought maybe I made a mistake and I thought she should be with me. I figured out later that it was best that she was not with me, but I still liked this poem. I know that one day I will have that special someone and I will have children, and one day he will run like I did down those stairs and that is when this poem will mean just a little more. I did finally give this poem to my ex-girlfriend and she really liked it. I think she still has this poem. I hope she ends up being happy and the man that ends up with her feels the same.

What I see
Is not always what I want
I look at what's in front of me
But I don't stop there
Only my heart knows
That you are what I want
Though you may not be in front of me
My heart never lets you leave
Some people keep trying
But no one can take my heart
Tonight I look straight ahead
Without focus
But I know with you I finally see clearly

A vision in the corner of my eyes
Like a video camera
Visions of you appear
Even if we are apart
You will always be with me
Though I can't touch the screen
I'll never forget
What I've seen
Hope to see you soon

When Dave's girl was away at school I couldn't stop thinking about her. I did not have any pictures of her, but I really did not need any pictures. She was always in my head. I could always remember the first day I met her and that picture never left my mind. I remember what she was wearing till this day. She was wearing shorts and a blue and white shirt. I don't think that will ever leave me. I know that she will always be there, but I will also remember that she was a step I had to take to get to be where I wanted to be.

No one can tell me
What I should do
No one can see inside
Everyone wants what I have
But do I still have it?
She doesn't know me
And that's what hurts
Two years and Im still alone
Everyday together
But still days away
I wanted her to know
But I am to late
I let her go
To find me
I want her
To see the inside
But she still sees the outside
Alone again
I want someone to explain
Giving a chance
But not taking

Still caught in the past
Looking for the future
Seeing what people have
One man and one woman
I don't need another
I love this one
And I hope she loves me
She told me Im the one
But I need to be sure

I wrote this poem when my ex-girlfriend and I were in a fight. She was just turning twenty-one and I got afraid that she would want the fun of being that age. I realized that I wanted her to be older, but that was not possible. We could have been a great couple if she was just a little closer to my age. We spent two years together and I thought she really knew me, but I was wrong. If she really knew me we would be together today. I could see the future, but I wanted it too much.

Does she walk
Where I have walked?
Does she feel
What I have felt?
Thinking about us
Telling myself she needs me
But hoping that Im right
Wondering what I did wrong

I wondered if she felt what I felt. Did she walk around wondering what she could do to get us back to where we once were? I would take long walks and wonder what I could do, but I always came up with nothing. I always felt like I was always in the wrong with her, and when you're with someone you should never have that feeling.

Please just hold me
I can't tell you why but please just do what I ask
I know that I have hurt you in the past
But all I am asking for is you to hold me
Nothing but you in control
I can't believe I am asking this of you
You can say no but please don't

I am lost and lost I will stay
Maybe more then lost I may be
These are big words but that's why I am asking for you to do this
I don't know what I am capable of
And there will not be anyone else in pain
And the pain I talk about wont last long for me
So please just hold me
You are in control of me, so I can get control of myself

I was having a lot of trouble with my family and I was not handling it that well. I needed someone to help me and I decided I needed a friend and that friend was there for me. I wrote what I wrote because I was not always there for her and she did not care. She just made me feel o.k. I think that everyone has those nights when they need someone and I was just glad that this person was there for me. I am still friends with this person and I think I always will be.

Where might she be
And how may she feel?
Tonight when she sleeps
Who will she think of?
I know she's not with me
But does she feel alone?
Though I might have someone else
She is the one I dream of
When my eyes are closed she is alive in me
I can feel her touch
And I can hear her voice
The smell of her perfume
Controls my senses
She talks to me in my dreams

I was dating a girl and I had this messed up dream. This girl that I knew was leaving and I guess I didn't want her to leave. I wondered if she felt the same as I did, because I knew I really felt a lot for her. I don't think I ever told her but I think she knew and we did not have a chance. It would have been fun though. One day she will read this and the secret will be out. I don't think it will change a thing but I will be happy to know that I told her. The Paula Cole song was on my mind.

Everything;
Its what you deserve
And its what I want you to have
I have given you my touch
I have given you my heart
I have given you my love
But tonight I hope I held back
I need to sit down as he speaks
I can't control my shaking body
My thoughts are of you
I hope he will tell me I kept this from you
Now do I hold you tight
Or do I hold back?
I will give you all of me that's what I told you
But tonight as I look at this man's blank stare
I hope I kept this
I've opened doors for you
I've given you roses
I've given you my life
But I don't want you to have everything
My heart is yours
My money is yours
And my love is only for you
So tonight I ask not only from this doctor
But from the man upstairs
I don't want you to have everything.

I don't know if you saw it, but I watched the press conference of Tommy Morrison. He was there with his wife and they looked lost. I could not imagine what they were thinking, but I wrote what I thought I would be thinking if I were in that situation.

Here I am wondering where and what you are doing tonight
He once had you under his control
Does he still have that power?
Tonight I am alone and he is with you
I told you it would be all right
For you to be friends with him

But I have a feeling that I am being a little blind
Things haven't changed but that does not mean a thing
In the beginning he was your friend and I was more than one
But is he more than one also.

When I was dating Dave's girl, Dave came to visit her. I told her at the time, that I did not care because I trusted her but I knew that I did not. That whole day I wondered if she was with him again. Dave's girl and I only dated for a few weeks and Dave came to see her. She dated him for three years and I knew that she still had feelings for him, but I also didn't want to get involved. I figured I would let her see him to see how much she wanted me. If I found out that she wanted him back I would leave, but if she realized they were done we could have a chance.

If I could reach any further
You would be in my arms
But my arms have lost some of their length
I'm afraid to open up
To many times they have reached for you
And you have pushed them away
Why should I care
Why should I love
And why should I cry
If I'm the only one with these feelings
Why do I want to be with you so much?
You have shown me what I thought were feelings
But what I have seen and heard are different tonight
If I meant so much to you
I would not be alone and you would not be with him
But tonight I am not alone as I walk around this town
I am not the only one that feels this way
My heart thinks he's all alone but my eyes see different
As I walk alone, I see others walking the same way

I can't believe that I am writing about this but I guess I will write about everything. You never really let someone know the whole you, someone asked me. I told them that is not true because I told Dave's girl everything, I thought. But tonight as I read what I once wrote I know that I didn't tell her everything. As I read this though I remember what it is to be hurt. I didn't know how much she hurt me until I read this poem once more. I found out months later, that she did cheat on me.

You say that my words touch your heart
Well I need my words to guide me
My words might have reached you
But I haven't found your heart
Hopefully my words will help me reach your heart
I want and need you to let your heart free
Let your heart and feelings touch my heart
How can my words touch your heart and I can't?

This was in my book from Kutztown. Some girl was reading my notebook and she even wrote me a little note. Her name was, "hope", and I actually wrote this for her. She enjoyed reading the poems in my notebook. I remember I let her borrow my music notes because she was sick. I used to write a lot when I was in class because my head would just wonder sometimes.

How many times have I done this?
I hope this time I really will go through with it
I know that I have sent a lot of letters but you have never seen them
The trash holds all that I want to say
I know that I told you that I cared for you
And I know that I told you that I love you
But there's no way you will know if I keep on throwing them away
If you felt like I did, you would know these things
But you want to be with another
I don't know how I do it but I do
I tell you over the phone that I am glad we are friends
I can't believe that you can't tell that I want more
You talk to him like he will be there forever
He may come and go as he pleases
But you tell him that you still love him
And that is why my trash is always filled.

I wanted more in this relationship as you can see. I thought this person could see this but I guess I was wrong. She and her new boyfriend did not last that long, and till this day my trash is still filled.

Not everyone understands
Though it hurts
We don't seem to notice

We say what we want
Because we are all in pain
Do we mean to cause pain?
Not everyone does
But pain is caused
I have heard you speak
Speak with anger
Holding back mine
May have caused me more
I listened then I hurt
Keeping it inside
Holding your anger
Understanding what you felt
And blaming myself
Your anger has died down
But stays alive in me
Though hidden it grows
Pushing you away from pain
Has pushed me away from you
Its time
Time for you to understand
Words that you have said hurt
Releasing your anger
Will release my pain
Then and only then
We will understand
What it is to listen
And it is to speak . . . .

I didn't know what to do. My dad and I got in our first true fight. We all get into arguments and we all won't always agree. I never got violent with my father though. I had a lot of anger towards him because of the comments he was making this night and the ones I remembered from the past. This night was not one of my best nights, and I knew that I took it out because I didn't let the past be the past.

You were once a thought and a dream
Then you became a friend and remained that dream
I wanted to tell you how I felt

The dream then became a reality
We became more then friends
Problems arouse
You no longer felt what I did
We parted and now you are the dream again
Now I look around and she is a thought
Will she become a dream
Will she become a reality
She may then become that dream
Is it all worth it . . . ?

One day I wondered if it all was worth it, actually I'm lying it's everyday. I don't think there is a day that I don't. One person that wants to be happy but this person hasn't found the real thing yet. I wrote this poem when I was at Kutztown, and just chatting with some people in my class. I think we were all bashing love that day. I may be unhappy right now but I am mistaking it definitely worth every second if you find the right one

A sight to my eyes
That's what you were
A feeling to my heart
That's what I felt
To see for the first time
I knew what I needed
And to hold you in my arms
That's what I wanted
You gave me a chance
You let me inside
I then became a sight for your eyes
And a feeling in your heart
We then made it forever
But today I wish I was blind
With his soft voice
He has changed our live's
I promised you everything
This sight to my eyes
Is not what I wanted
A collapse of your heart
Is a weight on mine

Forever will come too soon
You gave me a chance
You let me inside
So much pain I have caused.

I wrote this poem after I saw this movie with John Travolta. [Phenomenon] if you have never seen it you must watch it. All movies touch people differently but I think this movie will touch anyone. I know it may be a chick movie for those tough guys but if you have ever wanted something bad enough you should like this movie. He wanted this woman since the day that he met her and he didn't stop trying. She didn't want to let him in but he found a way.

The smell
Has not been forgotten
The touch
Has been missed
And the sound never leaves me
Your body is not where it used to be
Because of that my heart has taken
A leave of absence
And my love for you will not go away
Why did I not realize
That you were my life?
Questions are all that I have
But only answers from you will bring us together
I tremble when I see the future.

My ex-girlfriend and I went our separate ways and I thought I was wrong. I prayed every day I would find a way that she would realize that I didn't want her to leave, but things were to far gone for us. We said a lot of hurtful things to each other. If you are reading this I hope that you will think about everything before you say it. One day it will come back to haunt you if you don't.

You talk to me through my dreams

Eyes open but my heart closed
I have given you what I wanted to give
But that's not how I should live

You talk to me in my dreams

Eyes blurred and heart open
You're giving and I'm receiving
I am almost there

I talk to you through my dreams

Eyes closed and my heart out
Im giving and watching you receive
We are now there

I want to listen to your dreams

How are your eyes, where is your heart?
Are you willing to give and how will you receive?
I want to know where you want to be

I always had dreams of the girl that I wanted. She would understand me like I understand her. I didn't want my ex-girlfriend and my relationship to end up like every other relationship. I let all of me show to her good and bad. I now realize that certain things should be hidden.

Girl One: Why? Just tell me that

Guy: The why I cannot answer. I know that you love me but it just does not Feel right. I do care about you but it just is not right for me. Please don't hate me. I just don't want to hurt you later.

Girl Two: Finally

Guy: Excuse me

Girl Two: It took you some time but you finally understand why I had to leave.

Guy: But that was different. I gave you everything you could ever need

Girl Two: And she did the same for you.

Guy: I guess you are right. I never thought I would hurt someone like you hurt me, but I can see that I was wrong. She loved me but it was not for me.
Our love was her to me not me to her. I do care for her but that was not enough and if I waited I would've caused more. I hope she sees that and does not see me as a man to hate.

Girl Two: Well, do you hate me?

Guy: No I could never hate anyone that I loved liked that. I thought we would be together forever.

Girl One: So did I

Girl Two: Now you will know that every love is not a true love. You might care but the love is not there. You both have to feel the same.

Guy: Will she forgive me?

Girl Two: Have you forgiven me?

Guy: It took me some time but I think I did. But I do find myself thinking of you sometime.

Girl Two: She will too.

Guy: I sometimes thought and hoped you will come back to me.

Girl Two: She will hope too.

Guy: I just hope she forgives me.

Girl Two: I always hoped that you didn't hate me, and I still find myself thinking about you. And soon you will find yourself thinking about her. It might be over for us but I want you to know that you were a good love even though you weren't my true love.

Every love is not a true love!

I used to listen to a lot of R&B music and I thought that one day I could write a song, about a relationship, well this was it. I guess I was wrong about my song writing ability.

Please tell me that I'm wrong
And tell me that you didn't forget you have me
I see your not crying or even feeling bad
I guess I am the only one that will cry tonight
Because I thought we had something
Something that I will never forget
You were the women for me
And I knew it since the first day
I knew that you didn't think you would fall for me
But I also didn't think, when I walked in the land of the southern belles.
I would be put underneath one girls spell.

When I found out that my ex-girlfriend from Mississippi called one of my friends while I was away I wrote this poem.
Found poem . . .

Every day goes by
I try to get you out of my mind
You told me it was over
But why can't I see it
We had something special
I thought we had something that would last
But you told me that you didn't want me hurt
If you didn't want me hurt
Then why did you leave
You knew that would hurt me more than anything else
Maybe you didn't know
Maybe I didn't tell you
But I can't live with maybes
You left me and I have to except that
You will never be back
But someone told me forever is forever
And you told me we would be together forever
That might not have happened

So I guess when you say you will never be back
Never might be something else
It may be awhile but to me I will wait

I don't know what I saw but it was some movie and I wrote.

Nothings changed
I still have the same questions
Why do I still care?
You have said it's over
But I'm still here lying to myself
I still think that we have a chance
Tonight as I whisper to myself that I love you
You are with another
Telling him the same
I know I should stop
But how can I stop forever
The chain of love
Has caught me
I'm all hooked up

I wrote this poem when Dave's girl was at school. This is when she left me the first time. I knew that she was dating other people and I was to, but I also knew that she meant a lot to me.
Old poem

Here I am again

When you need me I'm there
I'm sorry but this has to be the last time
I can not keep catching those tears without caring
This is not fair to me
He has hurt you once again
And I am helping you
It first starts with the phone
I listen to what you have to say
I then come over to hold you
And dry away those tears
We then start to laugh and enjoy the friendship we have

You said you wanted to die on the phone
But hours have past and now you want to go out

I was just about to go out with my sister and one of her friends and I received a desperate phone call one of my ex's crying. They needed me to come and talk to her, because I was the only one that she could talk to. She wanted me to listen and not to talk, but I realized I started to feel for her.
Old poem . . .

To be here
Where I was raised
What should feel like home
Doesn't
Home to me is with you
That is the place where I want to be
You told me you don't feel the same
Maybe its because we've been apart for so long
That might be the reason you say you don't care
Well I'm making a change
I am taking a chance
The miles that we are apart won't be miles
Soon I will be right next to you
So you can tell me you don't care to my face
Because my ears don't believe the words you speak
When I see your face then I will know
How you feel
It is true, seeing is believing

When Dave's girl left for school I knew that we would be over but I didn't really know. I actually didn't want to believe it. I remember I sat outside of my house under the front light. I could not believe how beautiful it looked outside. It looked like a movie set. There were leaves on the ground and they looked so good they looked placed. I sat there for a couple of hours writing down exactly what I thought of everything and everyone.
Old poem . . .

Tonight I feel
What I should've felt sometime ago
I hear you cry and tears are loud

He has said good-bye
And this time he means it
You and him are finally through
You might ask why I think your tears are loud
Sometime ago before we became friends
I did the same to you
I did not hear you when I hurt you
I wish I would've
Then the pain I feel tonight would not hurt as bad
Tonight I know you feel pain but you don't know how
Much it hurts me

My friend broke up with Eddie. Actually Eddie broke up with her. My friend called me and she cried for an hour. I couldn't help but think back on the day that we broke up. I did not even bother to listen to her tears. I remember that her brother called me that day to ask me what was going on, because my friend would not come out of her room. She just told him to leave and just ask me what was wrong. I will never forget what a jerk I was that day. I just hope she has forgotten.

I received something tonight
I should have received a long time ago
I cant believe it took me this long
But tonight I hurt
He has hurt you
And your tears are killing me
But I will not tell you why
I will try my best to comfort you
The reason I hurt, is because I did the same
Before we were friends
I was the one that made you cry
But your tears I did not hear
To hear you tonight makes up for not hearing you before.

Thursday, Jan 2

I wrote this in my journal that night. Tonight my friend called me up and told me Eddie broke up with her. She was in tears I knew she was hurting, but also hurt me, which I deserved. When we broke up it didn't bother me. Well I can't say that it didn't bother me at all. But I didn't feel what I feel tonight. Eddie hurt her but I did the same. Usually I could help people when they feel down, but tonight I couldn't I didn't help her at all. I couldn't even help myself. I guess you can say tonight finally opened my eyes. This is something that should've been opened a year ago.

Now I'm here
My head is straight
When I looked into his eyes I knew
His pain gave me a reason to lose mine
He needs my help
Yesterday I was thinking about a short route
But today no way
How can this be
Sometimes pain, changes me
Maybe I see me in him
I don't know
But he won't be alone
That I know . . .

I was over at my girlfriends house one night. I must say an ex-girlfriend and her younger brother were having a rough time of it. I must have sat with him for an hour, and listened. I never really thought anyone in so much pain could help me, but he did . . .

Last night I found something we both lost
I found the time
The time that we shared
It was in my heart
And that is were it will stay
Unless you love me
Love me like you used to
Oh yes it is on my heart
And from me it will never part
I put it deep
Deep where no one can see
Then no one will know
Know how much you hurt me

It was the fourth of July and I had just returned from picking up Dave's girl from Millersville. I talked to her when she was at school and she told me that she was spending the fourth alone at school. I felt bad so I drove up to Millersville and picked her up. I wanted her to enjoy the holiday. I can't believe I did it though. At that time she really didn't give me a chance. I felt like I was something to do.

Old poem . . .

All my dreams have you in them
Everything is perfect
Me with you dancing
Holding you tight
Then later that night
Like I said everything was perfect
The way I described you to my friends
They thought you were
I wanted my friends to think I was happy
But all things I said came from a dream
And my dreams never come true
But wait we did have some good times
But I think time has made them better then they were
Sometimes I wonder why I make you look so good
Then I remember. To me, you were
Than time, showed you in a different life
And you're forever past
That's where you hurt me
It was like a two way mirror
You could see my love but I didn't see yours
And now that I look back
Did you actually have love for me?
Well it does not matter now
We have made up our minds
We will try somewhere else to find love
But as I look back tonight
I really would have liked to see my dreams come true.

I thought of Drea a lot when I did not see her. I thought that maybe I had made a mistake. I wished that I could go back again to change her mind. If it weren't for

Cougar I would have gone back about a thousand times. I didn't understand but I did find out and the hard way. Drea was not the one for me.
Old poem.

Almost lost
Where she may be
Everyone wants to know
Who will ask next
Don't they know?
I guess not
Tonight I will find
With a little help
Almost I lost
There she stands
Then a smile she gives
That's something I couldn't forget
Away with my fears
I gave her a hug
Holding my tears
And I see she does the same
A smile she gives
Hiding her fears
I tell her my thoughts
This won't be forgotten
I lost than I found, than lost
A step back she takes
Afraid of my plans

Though my ex-girlfriend and I broke up we still spent a lot of time together and this is what I wrote.

Time
It has shown me life
I still care a great deal
But I have seen we can never be together again
I know I have made a few mistakes
But time has also shown me
That my love for you will never change

I still think of the times we shared
I wish that I had never made the mistakes I made
I miss holding you in my arms
And telling you that I love you
The reason why I say that we can never be together, again is life
My life has brought me to a place I didn't want to be in
You deserve better than my life
Just remember in my life I did and always will love you
And I will never regret my life because of that

This was one of my first poems for my first real girlfriend. Her and I enjoyed being together but we were worlds apart in certain ways.

I try
But does it work?
I show
But do you notice?
I hold
Because I want to
And I kiss
Because I love to
I don't know all the answers
And I still have questions
The who
I think is you
The what
A feeling that feels strange
The where
Every place you are
The when
At this moment
The how
Is the biggest question
I try
I show
I hold
And I kiss
But is that enough?
You are my answers
And I want to be yours

I remember one night that my ex-girlfriend and I were fighting she told me that I never answer her questions. I sat back that night and I answered them all. I know that I didn't give this to her, but today I answered them for her to see. Every question is answered and no one should have any questions. I explained how I feel and the only thing is needed his her answers.

Can I find
Where to grab
There's nothing to hold
Is it you
Water surrounds me
Scared of drowning
Love is tricky
Taking so little
But giving so much
It goes both ways
Holding on to you
Not so secure
But feeling strength
What's next
No one knows
Tomorrow will come
But what does it bring
You and I
I really don't know
Wishing the same
I daydream at night
In my sleep
My dreams show only you
Nothing in our way
To easy they say
I really don't care
It's my dream
The dream I want
Not only in my sleep.

I don't remember the day or the night I wrote this. I just remember what I was doing when I wrote this. I was dating my ex-girlfriend and she was fast asleep. I remember that I just watched her sleep and I couldn't take my eyes off of her, but I kept on dozing off. I know that I was tired, but I wanted one more look at her before

I went to sleep. I know that tomorrow I would see her there, but I wanted to keep looking. I didn't know where our relationship was going, but I know I didn't want her to go far from me. She was all that I wanted and I wanted her to know that.

Can you
If I ask
Will you
When I need
Questions are all I have
And the answers are what you have
Not seeing you is slowly killing me
But to you life just went on
Do you
Like I do
Will you
Like I would
I have no idea how you feel
And you don't even know that I love you
You said nothing when I left
But you also don't know why I had to leave
If I told you
Would you care
When I talk
Would you listen
I have to see you
And I have to be with you
You are what I need
But I need to know if you feel the same.

I don't understand why people have to give so much to one day loses it all. I thought I really needed to be with this girl and I needed to know if she felt the same. If I found out that she felt the same I thought all my prayers would be answered. Old poem . . .

Time does not change
And time does not slow down
We look for the seconds
And hope the hours

Two people together
We look for the years
And only have time
For the minutes
One day we'll look back
And remember these minutes
The day all our friends
Will see how beautiful
You look in my eyes

On November 9, 1996 my sister kelly was married. She asked me to write her a poem for her bookmarkers. Her wedding song was by Joshua Kadison; you look beautiful in my eyes. So I put that in the poem.

I was told that I never hurt
I end it before its time
I don't let anyone to close
This maybe true
But I could be right
I don't know what maybe
But I know what is not
Only time can tell
But my clock has stopped
I will let it run again
But I will control the hands
I can stop what is broken
And start it again
To find what works
Is what I need
And one day I will give my hand
For one to hold
Till the day my heart stops

I heard people talk about me one day at work and this is what I had to say about that. I think they really thought they knew what I was about, but they were wrong. I know that I might come of a certain way, but I just want something that will stay. I am like everyone else that is looking to find someone that will care for them the same way.

Everyone can tell you
That I am not the one
Everyone can see
That you deserve better
They tell me I should let you go
Because you need me to
But do they really know
That you are my life
And that I am yours
One day I will hold your hands
With one knee on the ground
For all to see
` What their eyes have missed
I can only be happy with you

My ex-girlfriend kept on telling me that her friends thought that she needed to get rid of me. I was no good for her, and that really started getting to me. She told me that she didn't care what they said, but I knew that in time it would matter. One day she would listen to all, and I would be left in the cold.

I can't see tomorrow
And today is unclear
Yesterday I went through
But I did enjoy the day before
That is when you was with me
And I was with you
Yesterday brought a change
And today has begun
If tomorrow hurts like today
I would like to skip it
I hurt like no one knows
The day before I had happiness
I can't go back
But I don't want to go forward
I want what I had

When I broke up with my ex-girlfriend I thought maybe I should try again. I don't think I ever broke up with someone and wondered why, but I did with her. I thought I should think again. I couldn't forget the good times that we had. I know that we had bad days, but they seemed to slip my mind more and more each day.

> **As I look around the room**
> **To all the faces that mean nothing to me**
> **I think back when you were one of those faces**
> **Oh, how time changes**
> **Now I will no longer see your face**
> **Because of the miles between us**
> **It seems difficult for me to find a face like yours**
> **I have seen a face, but that face belongs to you**
> **I can't believe how much this hurts**
> **I have to be stronger**
> **I want to look for another face**
> **A face that will make me happy as yours did**
> **But this time I hope it will last longer**
> **So their face does not become a dream like yours**

I think it is amazing how you meet someone and they don't seem like they will mean anything to you and one day you realize they are. I always look around and wonder what someone can be to me. I think that is why I am so picky. Though someone may be beautiful to someone else I see the whole picture.

Old poem . . .

> **We say that we have forgotten**
> **But as we look into someone else's eyes**
> **And we tell them that we care**
> **Have we really forgotten**
> **Cause I know in my heart**
> **There is still something there for her**
> **I told her that I would love her forever**
> **And she always will be apart of me**
> **I have not changed**
> **She is still apart of me**
> **She is the part that brought me to you**
> **I know that you had him**
> **And he is a part of you**
> **That is the part that brought you to me**

Can we get over that
I don't know
But I am willing to let go
If you are willing to go

My ex-girlfriend told me one day that she could not get past my past. That made me think and I wondered if I could get past her past. The end result is clear I could, but she could not. Everyone that someone has dated in their past has made them the person that they are today. I didn't think that was bad, but every day that passes I wonder if it is. I am building walls that I never thought I would. I know that some will make me smarter but some will make me less. I never minded to trust, but today I learned not to trust all the time.

I could close my eyes
I know tomorrow is next
But today is what I am worried about
She has missed everything
Someone else knows
What I wanted only her to know
Everyday passes
With her away from me
One day we will meet
Which I will tell her about today
She will wish she was there
And today I wish she was too

When my ex-girlfriend and I broke up I was afraid of what she would miss. I was afraid to do anything fun or good. I didn't want her to miss anything in my life. If I did do something I wanted to call her and tell her just so I could hear what she thought. I think that is when I realized that we were truly done. The happiness that I remember was no longer there.

I know the first few are rough
But I know that I must
If I don't I will be caught
Caught and never let go
Hoping to be together
But always will be apart
Two people hoping for love

But only finding hate
I must walk alone
Giving all I got
And her doing the same
Hoping that we will connect
But finding us all alone
Holding on to forever
When forever is not there
Two people hoping it will work
But only showing anger
We must walk alone
Left then right
My feet are moving
I can't turn back
There is no about face
I can be apart
Hoping to find another
One person looking for love
But only seeing his past
I will walk alone
To find the one that walks for me

Jan 30 1999

I tried my best to do what was right, but I always came out in the wrong. Holding onto what was slowly killing me. I wanted to make right what was wrong, but I couldn't. I finally figured out that I had to move on to find again. To look to my future and bury my past.

I thought I knew what I was doing
But you and I together have no idea
What we are getting into
The friends I have look at you as you are free
To me you are not
But I have not made that clear
I tell you that I care and that I enjoy being in your arms
But then why don't I make you mine
Why am I holding back on something I know that I want
If I could explain my feelings to you in words
As they are in my thoughts

I have a feeling we would have something
Something that will make both of us happy

I took a look at what I know that I wanted and I realized I didn't have it. I can see this person without seeing her. She is in my thoughts. I told my friends that the girl that I was seeing was just another girl. My friend told her about my three-month rule. When I dated people in my past it was for three months. I thought was the best thing to do. I always thought you could tell by that time what you really thought of that person by then. The first two months were always good, and the third month they would start to show their true colors. I guess I got that I got that from baseball, one, two, three, and you are out.

**I know it should be easy
But I can't seem to do it
I've done it every night
I just lay down
And close my eyes
I wish it was that easy
If you were here it would
But you are away
With a little help from me
Letting you go
Might be my problem
I said I couldn't take us anymore
But tonight I can't take us, not
I didn't know what I wanted
But know, I know what I don't**

I know that I helped my ex-girlfriend leave me. One day I hope I will realize if I was right, but this day I thought I was wrong.

Hiding from you

**I can tell them all
That I feel nothing
But I know me
I can see you in my sights
You are there
Holding me in your arms**

Hiding from you
Holding back from what I feel
I know that I should
And I know that she has
Where to go next
Do I really want to
Taking time off
Not needing someone
And wanting one
Confusion sets in
Give up to gain
I hear those words
This is what I have done
But I did not gain
What I gave up was to much

I listen to, to many people that is what I think. I hear people tell me if it is meant to be it will. I heard one person tell me you have to give up to gain. You may feel hurt now, but things will change. If you let the bird go and it comes back to you then you know that it was truly yours. At this moment in my life I don't believe any of that. I know that right now it is hard for me to understand that, because I have too much invested in the love that I just lost.

Changing
Seeing what once was
And now no longer
Falling in love
Has now fallen apart
She was my life
But now she is not
Have I changed
Or has she
I still feel the same
But I have lost
Lost my love for her
She is gone
Gone where I don't want to be
Growing old with her
Changed to just growing old

I was starting to take a long look at what once was and I realized I never had it. Everything that we talked about was a lie. We thought we could be friends, but we soon came to realize that we could not. She was looking straight in my face and telling me lies. I think in a way so was I. I didn't realize it until it was to late. We could not go back and I realized I might just grow old and not find that special someone.

I want what I once laughed about
But now I wonder
I see him touch her
With that special something
Everyone seems to have it
That makes me feel alone
My brothers and sisters have it
But I have to give up
I've tried
And it's not there
I can't find it
I search and search
And I'm still alone
I have given
But I have not received
Tonight I need myself
To pick me up
Giving up will be hard
But I must
I can't take this
Not everyone can find it
I must move on

Time and time I told myself I must give up and find someone that feels the same way I feel. This day was different; I needed to stop thinking that way. I was in a relationship that was not for me.

I know who I am
And soon you will too
Holding back what I feel
Just waiting for my time
Watching one hurt you

Has hurt me
I know what you wanted
You needed to know
You thought he would stay
But he is not the one
I have known this
He can not give it all
When you cry he is not there
I don't think he even knows why you cry
When you are happy
I don't think he is happy for you
When you want to be loved
I don't think he knows how
My time is now
I need to be seen
For us to be together

I was taking a look at someone relationship and I realized I wanted what he had. I did not think he knew what he had with her. She was always there for him and he wasn't always there for her. I knew this, because she would talk to me and tell me. I would sit and listen to her and I couldn't stop thinking she should be with me. Her and I had the same thoughts and feelings.

One day all my dreams will come true. Everything happens for a reason and that is what I tell myself. Anyone that I have dated in my past was not meant for me. There is still one out there. Each day I feel that my sister was right by calling me the 'instant love pup'. Right now I am sitting in the Dallas airport just looking around and wondering. I met two girls from Birmingham, Alabama. I just stopped and thought maybe one of them could be the one. I'm also looking right in front of me and there is a girl reading a book. I ask myself does she feel the same way I do, because I see her looking around. Maybe she has someone, in my opinion she should have someone. Everyday I get antsy about my future. Is she out there and when will she come. Last week I even got a tattoo; it's chinese and it means, 'destiny'. It's the only thing right now that makes me believe it will happen.

I've been walking through my life
Waiting to see my future
My eyes have been closed
But my heart has been opened
I thought

When we think about our future
We wish for things to change
We might even hope for that someone special
But what will our future bring
We all want to know
But we will not find out till tomorrow
We think
So we all fall asleep and wait
But is anyone paying attention
Your dreams can be your future
Use your dreams
And find that someone special
Just don't be afraid to act
They might have that same dream

I wrote this because I knew that I have looked at some people and wondered. I could see that they did the same but I was afraid to try.

At first I was asking just because
I then asked because I enjoyed the first one
When I asked again, I knew I was looking for more
But when you asked I felt sure
I didn't think anymore
I usually wonder how a women feels
But you answered me
By asking me for the next dance

I really enjoy dancing but I am always afraid to ask for the dance.

You are talking to me in my dreams
You are a beautiful sight
You are my angel
You told me my future
You told me about a change
You told me to keep it quiet
You gave me hope
But that was in my dreams
The day is now here
Now I look at you

I see the same
You still have that light
You are my angel

I decided I needed some help with my future. I looked deep and looked to my dreams. I saw something that made me think. She saw what I could not. I wanted everyone to see what I saw, but she told me to hold it in. Only her and I could see what would and could be.

Close them
Then open them
One piece of skin
That controls so much
During the day it stays open
During the night it's closed
I can see you
All day and night
You have the control
To keep me awake
And to put me asleep
I can't seem to close them
When you are around
And I don't want them opened
When I see you in my sleep

I met this girl that just wanted to be friends. We would talk for hours about her life and mine. We were friends that would talk about our bad relationships and what a person would have to do to improve. She was always in my thoughts day and night. I wanted to call her before I fell asleep and I wanted to call her when I woke up.

She walks by me
I can see what she could be
She passes me in her car
Maybe she is the one
I see her on TV
When will I meet her
No one knows how it happens
But it does
Has she been in my life

Have I left her behind
One day we will meet
But I don't know today
I would like to find out
I feel love growing
For someone I do not know
Will it be soon
Or will I be old and gray
I believe in it
I am the instant love pup

My sister called me the instant love pup and she was right. I couldn't help to think that everyone that I met could be the one.

What can I do
Without hurting one
How can you notice
With just a couple of words
I can see what I want
If you and I were one
I wouldn't have to think
I would know
I've kept this to myself
But others have noticed
That you are more
More than I can say
I only have one look
When I see you
No one else is there
Even in a crowd
I try not to hurt him
And I hope he doesn't notice
But I know
That you are what I need
He may have
But does he know what he has
I whisper to myself
That he has my life

But I keep this inside
Maybe one day
He will be gone
So I can show you
What I have for you

After hanging out with my friend for a few days I realized that all the bad relationships that she had I could of done better. I knew what she wanted and I could be the one to make her happy. But I didn't think it was the right time.

Words from my heart
Are written for all to see
Holding back nothing
Letting my feelings show
Only to be alone
One day all this will change
Someone will come
Understanding where I come from
And letting me hear her words
Words that will bring us together

I looked at all the words that I have written, and wondered if anyone would really understand them. I was hoping that one day someone would read this and they would realize that they have been doing the same.

When I woke up
All my dreams were over
My day had started
But my dream reappeared
I saw my dream
You walked into my eyes
Not knowing if I was asleep
I looked up at the sun
The sun told me I was awake
But your sight told me I was alive
Wanting to show you all of me
But holding back
Waiting to see your response

My friend I would talk for hours and not realizing the time, I woke up in her arms. That day I realized she was becoming more than a friend.

You brought me here
But what does that mean
I don't know where here is
Tomorrow is not here
We talked about it
But it was different
You and I were together
But together we are not
What happened
Did I take the wrong turn
I didn't know I needed a map
To find my future

I found out that I was not the only one in someone's life. We were together but I was the only that thought that.

What I can be
Is what makes you scared
What I see
Is what you can't be
If it was possible
I could be what you will want
Time is stopping us
What you need today
Is not what I am
What you'll need tomorrow
Is what I am
I can't wait
My needs are important
I want what I see
But I have to see the real you
You are afraid
Afraid of a kiss
That can change you
I see it in your eyes
You want what I am
But not today

I can see what you want
But you ask if I could hold off
Hold off till tomorrow
You want that kiss
But you are afraid
Afraid of what may happen
Today you just need
Tomorrow you will want
You need to feel free today
But you like what I am
That kiss is important
It controls our future
It maybe the one you've been looking for
Or it could end your dream
I've been there for you
And I see your future
But today I need mine
Today is the day
I will go for that kiss
That leds to tomorrow

My friend and I had been friends for a while and I wanted the relationship to move on but she was afraid. She told me that she was afraid that I could be the one and that she thought she wasn't enough for me. She thought I could do better and I told her she was wrong. I wanted to move on.

The sun is like my heart
It releases rays for you
When you feel the heat from the sun
You are able to feel me
It's almost like the touch of my hands
My eyes on you, will never leave
The clouds may cover
But you know it's still there
The night falls and the sun can not be seen
Will you see me tomorrow
If the sun is out you will
The sun and I are connected
Able to be seen by you gives me energy
Energy to shine forever

I was at work and someone had a picture of a sun and a hand. I asked to borrow it for a second because it gave me this thought.

I started with twelve
But you will only receive six
She loves me
She loves not
She loves me
She loves me not
I only kept the ones that say you love me
I don't want you to have to think
Because I know I do not have too
You have talked to me in my dreams
You have showed me a change
You have showed me that you are the one
Some people say that dreams never die
But I'm glad mine have
Sleep is no longer necessary
I would rather stay awake
And look into to your eyes
So I can see the real thing
A dream without sleeping
Karen weaver, you are my angel
With you I don't need dreams

I brought my wife, actually girlfriend at the time, six roses one time. I meant to give her this poem with the flowers but I left the poem at home. I ended up given her the poem a few months later and then she understood the flowers more.

For my wife

The struggle of just one
Has become the struggle of so many
Watching the hands clench
With the body shaking
And the face tighting up
Asking for one more push
For the twenty-second time
Finally the struggle had ended

One has been born to us
But my struggle has just been realized
What we have done for her
My parents have already done for me
Taking advantage of what I have been given
Was not my intention
But it is my struggle this day
Did my parents realize this
This struggle of one
Has opened so many thoughts
But one is more important than all the rest
This struggle will never be forgotten
Life has been given to me from all sides
Past, present, and future has been seen
I did, I do and always will love you

I thought I was never going to find this thing called, love. I thought I would always write about it and talk about it, but I never thought it would come. The day I saw my wife come down that aisle in front of all my friends and family I thought I found it. But this day made me think that love has no limits. When I saw my wife reach for her baby and mine. I then realized I still have more to learn. I did not think it was possible that I would become more in love with my wife, but this day proved me wrong. She told me numerous times before we had our baby how scared she was about having this baby, but this day I did not see how scared she said she would be.

Looking at her today I love my wife all over again and I love my baby just as much.

Never say never

Today and every day, I will be reminded of this
Never say never
I look in her eyes
I thought it would never happen
I told all my friends
I made myself believe it was true
I would never be happy and in love
But you did come

I thought I could never be happier
Never say never
When will I learn
You and I made something
That made me happier
She was given to us
And I am afraid to say it once more
One day I will learn
Never say never
Today I have come up with something new
Never say never will be lost
Always and forever will take its place
That is how long I will love you both
You and our baby have given me so much
So, always and forever is what I will give you

I look at my six year old daughter today as I read what I have written in the past and I realize that these poems brought me to her and her mother. If I could change anything, I would take out the heartache but I know that is not possible. I would hope that she does not go through as much, but this is a way to show her that her dad went through it and I know that she will too. She will be strong enough and hopefully smart enough to see what is real and what is not. (Maybe even better then dad) I hope that one day she will be as lucky as I have been and end up with a wonderful baby. Times will get rough but things will work out.

In love with the ring

In love with the ring
knowing what was there
thinking of what has happened
not knowing what is in front of you
the possibilities are endless
going through everything together
one piece of jewelry
never meant so much
scratches and bends on it
but still firmly attached
in love with the person
the person that sees the same thing

in love with the rings
years together leaves a mark
the finger will never be the same
the indent on the finger
is now visible to all
in love with the ring
that now fills the drawer
the drawer that holds just junk
still in love with the ring
and it's possibilities
not in love with the indent
the possibilities have ended
the ring is just junk
the scratches will always be there
the years will never be forgotten
the ring will soon be lost
lost what made it feel special
no longer in love with the ring
that made me feel happy.